Contents

Words that appear in **bold** can be found in the glossary on page 30

Where are you?

Maps help you to find out where you are. A map is a picture of a place drawn from above – as a person would see from the window of a plane.

Most maps published by the Ordnance Survey are covered in a grid. This grid, like the one below, helps you to describe where you are. Vertical lines that go from West to East are called Eastings. Lines that go from South to North are called Northings. Northings and

Eastings are numbered. To give your location on a map, give the number of the Easting line closest to your left, followed by the Northing line directly South of you. If you are at X in the grid below, your 4-figure grid reference is 0212.

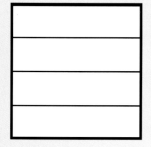

Northings

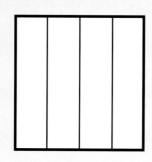

Eastings

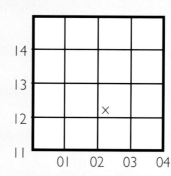

The numbers for Eastings are along the bottom. The numbers for Northings go up the side.

Can you give a four-figure grid reference for the following features on the map?

A hotel

A caravan site

A tourist information centre

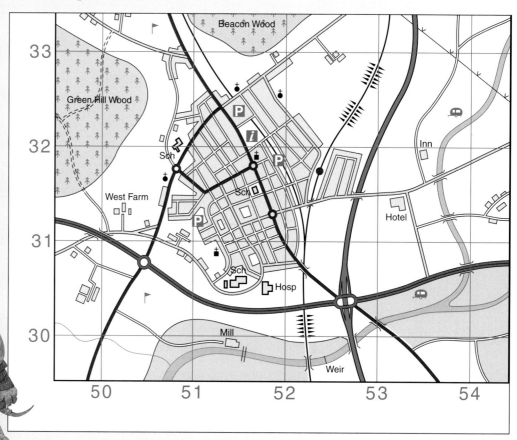

THE GEOGRAPHY DETECTIVE INVESTIGATES

Your Local Area

Ruth Jenkins

WAYLAND

Other titles in The Geography Detective Investigates series:
Rivers

First published in Great Britain in 2006 by Wayland, a division of
Hachette Children's Books
338 Euston Road, London NW1 3BH

This paperback edition published in 2008 by Wayland,
a division of Hachette Children's Books

Editor: Hayley Leach
Designer: Simon Borrough
Maps and artwork: Peter Bull
Cartoon artwork: Richard Hook
Consultant: John Lace

British Library Cataloguing in Publication Data
Jenkins, Ruth, 1978 –
   Your local area. – (the geography detective investigates)
   1. Local geography – Juvenile literature
   1. Title
   910

ISBN 978 0 7502 5512 7

Picture acknowledgements.
The publishers would like to thank the following for permission to
reproduce their pictures: akg-images 7 (left) (British Library); Alamy 9 (Mike
McEnnerney), 11 (bottom), 14 (Photofusion Picture Library), 28 (David
Sanger Photography), 15 (left) (Kathy deWitt); Corbis 10 (Ashley Cooper), 5
(Mousis Francois), 21 (bottom) (Chinch Gryniewicz), 26 (Angela Hampton),
23 (left) (Ian Harwood; Ecoscene), 21 (top) (Jason Hawkes), 12 (Helen King),
title page and 7 (right) (London Aerial Photo Library), 13 (Richard Morrell),
24 (Reuters), 8 (Ted Spiegel), 12 (William Taufic), cover and 6 (Patrick Ward),
23 (right) (Terry Whittaker; Frank Lane Picture Agency); Ecoscene 22 (Frank
Blackburn), 17 (top) (Vicki Coombs), 29 (top) (Lorenzo Lees), 27 (Sally
Morgan), 16, 29 (bottom) (Ray Roberts), 17 (bottom) (Jim Winkley); Wayland
Picture Library 15 (bottom) 25 (top and bottom).

Maps come in a variety of sizes or scales. The scale shows how much each unit of distance on the map represents in the real world. The scale is sometimes shown as a representative fraction such as 1:50 000. This means that one centimetre on the map represents 50,000 centimetres in the real world. Scales make maps easier to use, as you can make maps any size you wish.

There are many new devices to make it easier to find your way. **Global positioning service** (GPS) **devices** communicate with satellites in space and are very accurate. Drivers in cars can use similar equipment to enable them to travel from one place to another without getting lost or stuck in traffic jams.

DETECTIVE WORK

Investigate different map scales using a pen, a simple map and a balloon. Take a pen and copy a simple outline map onto the surface of a deflated balloon. Blow the balloon up. As the balloon becomes larger, the scale of the map changes and the detail on your map becomes easier to see.

You can find maps and photographs to show your local area on the Internet. To find out more, go to:

weblinks

www.waylinks.co.uk/series/
GeogDetective/LocalArea

The sailor Ellen MacArthur training for a race on her yacht, *Kingfisher*. Ellen depends on global positioning service (GPS) devices to navigate accurately around the globe.

How would you describe the landscape around you?

A landscape is an area of land or the place around you. Your landscape will vary depending on where you live: in the countryside or in a town. If you live in a town, the landscape will be affected by things that people have built, such as houses, offices, shops and roads. We use several tools to help us describe the landscape around us.

A quiet countryside village in the Yorkshire Dales.

Drawing a picture of a landscape will help you to describe it. Why not make your own drawing or sketch? The view from your bedroom window would be a good place to start. Try to include as many details of the place around you as you can. When drawing, look at your landscape very carefully, but limit your sketch to a small area so you can draw every detail that you see. Sketching helps you notice things that you would miss if you just took a photograph.

Maps give us a picture of the landscape around us. They help us to see how close things are to each other and they help us to find our way from one place to another. Before we had satellites, photography and aeroplanes, people drew maps by hand. This meant that maps were not always accurate. Certain countries, such as America, were not included on world maps because they had not been discovered! Other places were sometimes marked in the wrong place, or areas seemed larger than they really were.

Look at the Mappa Mundi map. What inaccuracies can you spot between this map and today's maps of the world?

An aerial view of busy residential roads in South London.

The Mappa Mundi was drawn during Anglo-Saxon times in around 1025. It is the oldest known world map found in Britain.

Landscapes differ depending on where you live. Towns and cities are built-up with houses, shops, schools and offices. This type of place is known as an **urban** area. The countryside is less built-up, with more land used for farming or parkland. Areas in the countryside are known as **rural** areas. Zones on the edge of cities, used mainly for housing are called 'suburban' – they are not as built-up as urban areas and many houses have gardens.

DETECTIVE WORK

Why not create your own map of your local area? Make your own map from an aerial photograph by putting a piece of tracing paper over the picture. Draw a line over the main features like roads, buildings or fields that you want to show. Lift your tracing paper away from you photo and you have a clear map! To view aerial photographs, go to:

weblinks

www.waylinks.co.uk/series/
GeogDetective/LocalArea

What's the story behind where you live?

A place where a settlement is built is called a **site**. The site where you live could have been built upon hundreds of years ago, or it may have only begun in the last fifty years. The age of some of the buildings in your area, especially churches or the town hall, will give you an idea of the history of where you live.

When settlements were first built, people thought carefully about where they picked their site. Several things affected their decision:

1 Water – People needed to be near to a safe supply of drinking water (a spring or a river). This supply could then be used for washing.

2 Building – People needed to be near a source of building materials so that they could build their homes – such as a forest for wood or a quarry for stone. Wood was also needed as a fuel for cooking and keeping warm.

3 Defence – If times were dangerous, people often built on high ground. This enabled them to see their enemies from a distance.

4 Fertile land – It was important to find land that was good for growing crops or grazing sheep or cows.

5 Transport – Rivers were used to move things from one place to another so that they could be swapped or sold. Transport is a very important factor influencing the site of new settlements today, as people need good roads to enable them to travel around easily.

Why not find out which of the factors listed influenced the people who chose to build where you live? The name of the settlement might give you a clue. Alternatively look on a map or walk around your area to see if you can see any of the factors nearby.

A directional sign in Norfolk, England. Town names with 'by' endings are evidence of Danish settlement in the area during the time of King Canute (c. 994-1035).

A view towards the medieval Corfe Castle and Corfe village, in Dorset.

People who live in certain places can sometimes be given nicknames. A person who lives in Newcastle-upon-Tyne, for example, is called a Geordie. Some people think that the people of Newcastle were given the name 'Geordie' for their support of King George II, in 1745. Others think that the name came from the name George Stephenson, who invented a lamp called the Geordie that was used by miners in Northumberland.

Someone who is born within 'the sound of Bow's bells', which belong to the Church of St Mary-le-Bow in Cheapside, East London are called 'Cockneys'. It is thought that the name started in the Middle Ages, when people from the city went to the countryside to find work. They weren't as healthy as those who lived in the country. At the time, if a hen laid an unhealthy or weak egg it was called a 'cock's egg'. As a result, the weaker people from London came to be known as 'Cokeneys,' which eventually became 'Cockney.' Why not find out if there are any nicknames for the people who live in your local area and see if you can discover the history behind the name.

Look at Corfe Castle and its surroundings. Can you think why Corfe Castle and Corfe village were built in this place?

DETECTIVE WORK

What's the story behind the name of where you live? The English and Scottish Place Name Societies will be able to help you find out about the origin of place names in England and Scotland. The Welsh Language Board might be able to help you discover the story behind Welsh place names. To find out more about the meaning of your town or village name, go to:

weblinks

www.waylinks.co.uk/series/ GeogDetective/LocalArea

How has the population of your area changed over time?

Over time, the people (or **population**) of a place can change dramatically. People move from one place to another – this movement is called migration. New people arrive from different places, adding to our **cultural diversity**. Many areas in the UK have a rich ethnic mix. An ethnic group is a community of people who might speak the same language, or practise the same traditions like going to church or eating certain foods.

Your local area is probably made up of children from many different backgrounds, like this group of young people in Leeds.

The Chinese Community

There is a significant Chinese community in London. Since the 1950s, it has been concentrated around the Chinatown area of Soho, near Leicester Square. China is an important trading partner to the UK – in 2005 there were over 250 international Chinese businesses in London. China's influence is felt in other areas of everyday life too – there are Chinese shops, restaurants, churches and health centres across the capital. There are also many Chinese students studying at London universities.

In some parts of the UK, such as the northeast, more and more people are moving away. Sometimes people leave a place to go and look for work somewhere else. In the UK, many people have moved southwards for this reason.

However, at the same time, some people are leaving large cities to go and live in the countryside in order to escape from crime, pollution and overcrowding. Sometimes people move away from the city when they retire to look for more peaceful surroundings.

The UK's population changes since 1981-2001

	1981 data	Population 2001	Change
North East	2,631,191	2,515,479	- 4.60%
North West	6,931,694	6,729,800	- 3.00%
Yorks/Humber	5,009,521	4,964,838	- 0.90%
East Midlands	3,838,405	4,172,179	+ 8.00%
W Midlands	5,185,028	5,267,337	+ 1.60%
East England	4,795,458	5,388,154	+ 1.00%
London	6,784,747	7,172,036	+ 5.40%
South East	7,168,493	8,000,550	+ 0.40%
South West	4,312,401	4,928,458	+ 2.50%

DETECTIVE WORK

Every ten years, a large survey of everyone who lives in the UK is carried out. This survey is called a census. The last one to be carried out in the UK was in 2001. To find out more information about the census in your local area, go to:

weblinks

www.waylinks.co.uk/series/
GeogDetective/LocalArea

Nurses at a hospital in London. The health service is an example of how people from many different ethnic backgrounds work side-by-side in the UK.

Ethnicity in England and Wales
(grouped by general background)

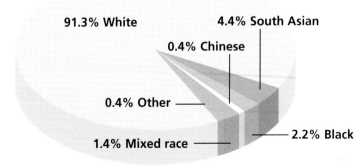

91.3% White
4.4% South Asian
0.4% Chinese
0.4% Other
1.4% Mixed race
2.2% Black

What do people do where you live?

People have to work to earn money. This work is called **economic activity**. There are three main types of economic activity that people in your local area will probably be involved in: primary, secondary and tertiary industry.

A tailor makes a suit using material to produce an item of clothing for sale. This is an example of work in a secondary industry.

A businesswoman talks to someone on the telephone in her office. The work she does is an example of a job in a tertiary industry.

Primary industry is all to do with producing things to eat and drink, or gathering resources that we use to make the things we need. Farming or forestry, where trees are cut down are two examples of primary industry. Secondary industry involves making things (known as manufacturing) from the materials or food we get from primary industry: making furniture from wood for example. Tertiary industry (also known as the service industry) involves jobs that provide a service for other people such as selling furniture or answering questions in a call centre.

In the UK, most people now work in tertiary industry, and the numbers of people working in primary and secondary industries has declined. Farming has become more efficient and machines have taken over much of the work that was done by people. Secondary industry has also become less important, as machines have taken over the work that people used to do. Many factories in the UK have shut down because it is cheaper to buy things that have been made in other countries, such as China, where the cost of human labour is much cheaper.

DETECTIVE WORK

What type of jobs do people do where you live? Carry out a survey in your class to find out more. Follow these steps to carry out your own survey:

1 Each person in your class should choose five adults to ask: What job do you do? Compare your results with your class.
2 Divide the answers into three categories. Use the table below to help you.
3 Decide which category each person's job fits into. Mark a tally in the correct column for each person.
4 Count the total number of tallies in each column. Which column has the most?

JOB IN PRIMARY INDUSTRY	JOB IN SECONDARY INDUSTRY	JOB IN TERTIARY INDUSTRY

This man is harvesting potatoes on a farm. The machine he is using means that the job can be done without the help of lots of other people.

How accessible is your local area?

Accessibility describes how easy it is for people to get to a place and to use the facilities that are there. **Accessibility** affects people differently. Some people might not be able to move around easily if they use a wheelchair, others can find it hard to navigate a busy road if they are partially sighted. Parents with prams might find it difficult to climb onto a bus.

We can use technology to make places more accessible. For example, most buses are fitted with ramps that make it easier to get on board if you have a pram or wheelchair. Forty-four out of London's 275 tube stations are step free, making them more accessible.

DETECTIVE WORK

How accessible is your area? Draw a map of your journey to school. Mark on the places where you cross the road or where you face obstacles. Imagine you had to make your journey using a wheelchair. How difficult would it be? Would you have to change your journey?

Trams in Sheffield are designed to cater for wheelchair access.

New inventions make crossing the road safer, especially for people who are disabled or for those who have trouble seeing properly. Some crossings have 'Walk Buttons'. These buttons stick out and give off two different noises. The red 'don't cross' sign is accompanied by a beep every two seconds. When it is safe to walk, there is a rapid 'pulsing' sound. This makes it easier for people to know when it is safe to cross the road.

'Walk-throughs' are built where there are no pedestrian crossings. They are like islands in the middle of the road and are safe places to wait for traffic to clear. They have ramps and handrails, to make it easier for people in wheelchairs to cross. Microwave detectors are fitted on top of traffic lights. They detect when someone is crossing the road, to ensure lights do not change suddenly.

Young women are waiting to cross the road at a set of traffic lights in London.

Look at the photograph of the two girls crossing the road. Can you work out what the bumps on the pavement are for?

Where does the food you eat come from?

People in the UK eat food from all over the world. Bananas from the Caribbean, tomatoes from Spain and lamb from New Zealand are not unusual, so the food that you eat can travel thousands of miles before arriving on your plate.

Food has never travelled as much or as far as it does today. Every journey that food makes – being taken to the supermarket to be sold or driven to peoples homes – damages the environment. This is because using the fuel that powers the cars, aeroplanes and lorries that transport our food contributes to **global warming.**

What can you do? Encourage your family to walk or take the bus to the supermarket instead of going in the car. Try to buy loose vegetables rather than those packaged in bags – they are less bulky, so need less fuel to be transported. Look out for local farmers' markets in your area, and buy food from people who grow food close to your home. This helps to reduce **food miles** which is the total distance an item of food has travelled.

Farmers' markets provide the chance to buy fresh produce directly from local farmers so that food does not need to travel too far.

DETECTIVE WORK

Next time you are going through the cupboards or the fridge at home, have a look at the labels on packets of food. Where in the world has all the food come from? Use an atlas to help you estimate the distance that your food has travelled.

People are also worried about chemicals on the food we eat. **Fertilizers** are used in farming to make plants grow faster and larger to help feed our growing **population**. Pesticides protect them from insects or mould. However, these chemicals can be difficult to wash off. Chemicals sprayed on fields can also build up in the soil or drain into nearby rivers, causing thick algae to grow. Algae removes oxygen from water, suffocating other plants and animals that live there.

Fertilizer use has decreased since the 1980s, but in the same period food production has increased. This tells us that farmers are using fertilizers more efficiently. Farmers have to be careful to apply fertilizers at the right time of year and in the right amounts. By doing this, fewer nutrients are washed away by the rain and more nutrients are absorbed by the plants for growth.

Some people believe that we should do more to encourage organic farming. Organic farmers aim to produce food without heavy chemical use. By changing the crops that are grown in fields each year, farmers can maintain the fertility of soil. Organic food is increasingly popular, but is more expensive than other produce, and organic farmers may struggle to produce enough food for our growing population.

These bananas have the Fairtrade logo on them. Fairtrade is an agreement that aims to pay farmers in Less Economically Developed countries (LEDCs) a fair price for the food they produce.

All these foods have been produced in an organic way.

What's the weather like where you live?

Weather is the typical conditions of the air around you at a particular time. The UK's position means that we have some of the most changeable weather in the world.

Weather in the UK is determined by the different **air masses** that meet over the British Isles. An air mass is a huge body of air that can extend for hundreds of miles. Different air masses affect our weather, and each air mass differs in temperature and the amount of moisture it contains. Air masses develop in large, flat areas of land or water in different parts of the world, such as Southern Europe or North Africa.

Different parts of the UK experience slightly different weather conditions as they are affected by different air masses:

- The northwest has cool summers, mild winters and heavy rain all year.
- In the northeast, summer and winter are cool: rainfall is constant across the year.
- Southeastern areas have warm summers, mild winters and light rain all year.
- The southwest has warm summers, mild winters and heavy rain all year, particularly in winter.

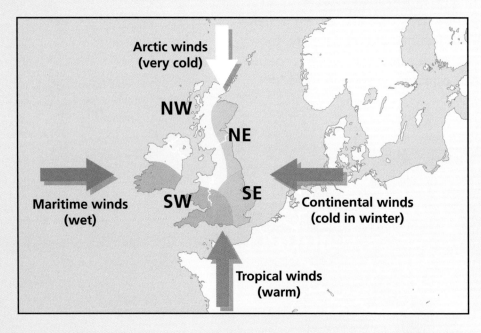

DETECTIVE WORK

5 million people in the UK are at risk of flooding because the amount of rainfall in the UK is increasing. Could you be at risk? To find out more go to:

weblinks

www.waylinks.co.uk/series/GeogDetective/LocalArea

This diagram shows how different air masses affect the weather in parts of the UK.

Climate describes the normal weather of a place over a long time. However, climate does not stay the same. Climate change is a natural process, but scientists tell us that people are making the Earth's climate change too fast. This is called **global warming**. It is caused by several gases, especially **carbon dioxide**.

Carbon dioxide is produced whenever we burn fossil fuels, such as coal, oil or gas, to obtain energy to power the things we use. Travelling in a car, flying in an aeroplane, watching television and heating your home all produce large amounts of carbon dioxide. This is contributing to something called the **enhanced greenhouse effect**.

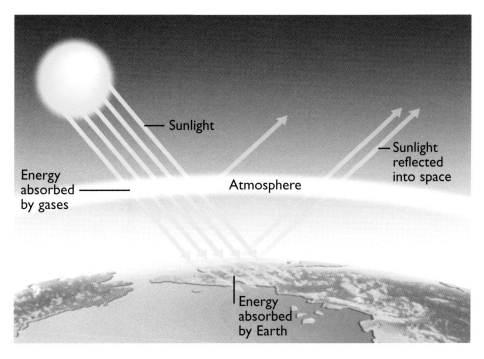

Sunlight

Energy absorbed by gases

Atmosphere

Sunlight reflected into space

Energy absorbed by Earth

Carbon dioxide in the atmosphere acts as a blanket around the Earth. This blanket traps heat, keeping the Earth warm, like a huge greenhouse. This process is normal, but now we are producing too much carbon dioxide, and the Earth is getting too hot.

FOCUS ON

Climate change in the UK

Global warming poses a threat to people, because it is thought to be behind extreme weather patterns. The average 10-year-old in the UK has lived through some of the country's most extreme weather ever recorded. The floods in Boscastle in 2004 are just one example of the freak weather thought to be caused by global warming. Global warming could cause sea levels to rise, and flooding could become more common. We can combat global warming by using less electricity, or cutting down on the amount we travel, so that less fossil fuel has to be burnt.

TRUE OR FALSE?
- Summer 2004 was the second warmest and third wettest since records began.

- Temperatures could rise by as much as 5°C in some parts of the UK by the 2080s.

- Flood damage could cost as much as 25 billion pounds by the 2080s.

Where does all the water come from?

Without water, we wouldn't survive. An average person needs 80 litres of water a day. In some countries, people use as much as 500 litres, others use much less.

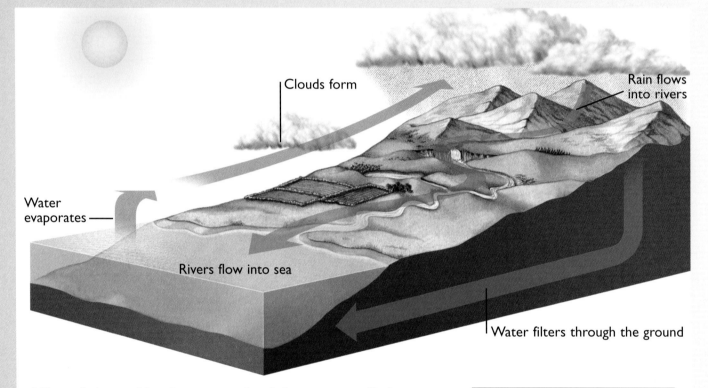

Clouds form

Rain flows into rivers

Water evaporates

Rivers flow into sea

Water filters through the ground

Water is heated by the sun turning it into a gas, called water vapour. As the air is cooled the water vapour forms into clouds. Rain from the clouds then falls over high land, forming rivers which flow back to the sea.

How does water reach your tap? The amount of water in the world never increases or decreases, it just moves around from one place to another, as either a gas, liquid or solid.

The water we use is taken from rivers and is stored in lakes called reservoirs. Some water is also pumped from underground lakes. Water is treated before we use it to remove dirt; it is then pumped into our homes.

DETECTIVE WORK

Not everyone in the world has access to clean water. A charity called Water Aid tells us that one billion people have access to only dirty water. To find out more go to:

weblinks

www.waylinks.co.uk/series/
GeogDetective/LocalArea

A reservoir in Scotland's Pentland Hills stores water ready for use in people's homes.

When you flush the toilet, waste-water is not washed straight into rivers. It is treated first. It passes through wire screens to remove solids. The water is then pumped into large tanks. This allows time for any particles of sand or sludge from the toilet to sink to the bottom. The liquid is treated again until it is clean enough to be pumped into rivers.

Across the UK, ten water companies supply our water. Underneath London, there are 20,000 miles of water pipes and 40,000 miles of sewers (pipes carrying waste-water) – that's enough pipes to circle the world twice!

Some parts of the UK, particularly in the southeast of England, experience periods of dry weather or droughts. This means that water supplies are low – the winter of 2004-2005 was the driest since 1976. The southeast of England experiences drier weather than the rest of the country, but it could also be partly to do with **global warming** (see page 19). During these times of drought people have to restrict their water use: using hosepipes is banned and some people choose to have a water meter fitted. This monitors exactly how much water is used. When you have a meter you are charged for the exact amount of water you use, so you tend to waste less of it.

FOCUS ON

Baths and showers

If 1,000 people had a shower each day instead of a bath, how much water would the UK save in a year? The answer is an amazing 16.4 million litres! An organization called Water Partners International estimates that an average African family uses 8,400 litres of water each year – that's almost less than half the amount one person in the UK could save by taking a shower rather than a bath.

The effects of drought are shown by cracks in the ground at Pentwyn Reservoir in Wales.

What else lives in your local area?

Y ou're likely to find lots of different animals living around you. Some are welcome, some are considered to be pests.

Nearly all cities have interesting wildlife. You can encourage birds to visit your garden by leaving food, water and boxes for them to nest in. If you don't have a garden, look in your local park. Early morning is the best time to spy animals before they have been disturbed by people. Overgrown plots provide perfect hiding ground for spiders, lizards and hedgehogs.

Most of the UK used to be covered in forests and woodland, but much was cleared for farming and building. Remaining pockets of woodland should be treasured and looked after. Forests are good places to visit, particularly early in the morning when you will hear loud birdsong.

Farmland is a good place to look for wildlife, but ensure you have permission. Farmland with old trees and hedgerows along the edge of the fields attracts lots of interesting wildlife.

DETECTIVE WORK

What animals do you have living in your garden or local park? Why not get involved in a project to encourage wildlife in your school playground? This could include making a pond or planting wild flowers. Find out more at:

weblinks

www.waylinks.co.uk/series/
GeogDetective/LocalArea

Hedgerows are important habitats for wildlife, such as this Red-backed Shrike who is feeding her chicks.

Some creatures can cause problems in your local area, especially if they carry disease. Seagulls are becoming a nuisance, especially in **urban** areas. In 2003, the city of Gloucester had 2,688 pairs of breeding black headed gulls, who have proven very good at finding food in the area. Seagulls block water pipes, damage roofs and foul areas with their droppings. They are thought to spread **e-coli** and **salmonella**, which cause health problems for people. Seagulls also costs airports up to £2 million a year, as runways must be cleared of seagulls before aircraft take off, to make sure that the birds do not hit the aircraft!

Numbers of urban foxes have increased dramatically, as they have learnt to adapt to an urban environment well. Can you think of any problems foxes cause in towns?

Rats

Rats are a huge pest, especially in **urban** areas. They can carry diseases like **Weil's disease**. Rats find plenty of food to eat in rubbish bins and sewers. Their sharp teeth are excellent for chewing through plastic, concrete and metal. This causes expensive damage and fires if electrical cables are damaged. Rats also breed quickly: a healthy female rat can produce five litters of 8-10 young, five times a year.

Seagulls hover over a landfill site in Portsmouth, searching for food amongst the rubbish.

How environmentally sustainable is your local area?

Sustainable development is about trying to improve problems in an area without damaging the things that are beneficial. The United Nations defines **sustainable** development as 'development that meets the needs of the present without compromising the ability of future generations to meet their own needs'. Problems in your local area could include dirty, polluted water, piles of rubbish that have to be buried rather than recycled and unclean air caused by fumes from cars and factories. Sustainable development is all about allowing people to have a better life today and in the future.

The congestion charge was introduced into London in 2002. Drivers now have to pay £8 if they wish to drive in parts of central London between 7am and 6.30pm.

How might the congestion charge help London to be more sustainable?

Travelling by bus is more environmentally friendly than travelling by car. Is there a local bus route that you could use?

DETECTIVE WORK

Most local councils have recycling schemes so that people can recycle things like paper, glass and plastic. Find out what your local council is doing to encourage recycling in your local area. The council's website will probably give you some of this information. To find out more information about getting involved in sustainable development, go to:

weblinks

www.waylinks.co.uk/series/
GeogDetective/LocalArea

People are trying to make the world a better place to live by taking local action to encourage sustainable development. This started after world leaders met in Rio de Janeiro in 1992. They agreed that people across the world need to work together to live in a more environmentally friendly way.

World leaders met again in Johannesburg, South Africa, in 2002, to review sustainable development's success. They agreed to ensure that all people had access to clean drinking water, to look after endangered animals, to generate more electricity from cleaner sources, such as wind and solar power, and to lower pollution levels. Part of this commitment has involved persuading people to **recycle** more waste and use more environmentally friendly forms of transport such as buses, cycles or by walking rather than using cars. The Rio Earth Summit's slogan was 'think global, act local': if everyone does their best to make their local area a better place, all of their efforts will come together to make the world a better place.

Recycling facilities can usually be found near your local supermarket.

How can you look after your local area?

Everybody has something called an **environmental footprint**. Your footprint is the effect your life has on the environment – like the amount of water you use or the rubbish you generate. You cannot get rid of your footprint altogether, but you can make it smaller.

At the moment, in the UK we use so much of the world's resources to live – for energy, food, clothes and transport – that if we continue to use these resources at the same rate, they will eventually run out. Since we only have one planet to live on, we have to look after it.

Looking after your local area is vital. Local Agenda 21 was a project set up after the United Nations conference in Rio in 1992 (see page 25). It encourages people to take action in their local area, to make sustainable development happen.

These people are staying healthy by using a bicycle for short journeys and they are helping the environment by not using a car at the same time.

DETECTIVE WORK

To find out how big your environmental footprint is, go to:

weblinks

www.waylinks.co.uk/series/
GeogDetective/LocalArea

Insulating your roof cuts heat loss from your family's house, reducing the amount of electricity used and saving money.

So what can you do? You can make a promise to make small changes to the way you live. Maybe you could walk to school instead of going by car or, if it is too far to walk, perhaps you could cycle. Persuade your parents to buy light bulbs that use electricity more efficiently so that you contribute less to **global warming** (see page 19). Simply making sure that you do not leave your television or video on standby will cut your electricity use. Make compost for the garden from your kitchen waste. Encourage your parents to make sure that your house is insulated properly so you don't lose heat through the roof. Not only will you use less electricity but this has the added bonus of reducing the bill for heating your home. You can make an even bigger impact by persuading friends to do the same.

Your school is another place where you can make a difference. Make sure lights are turned off in empty classrooms. Encourage your school to set up **recycling** schemes. Maybe you could even set up a wildlife garden in your school grounds.

FOCUS ON

Light bulbs

If you replaced two of the bulbs in your home with energy saving light bulbs, you would prevent 40 kg of carbon dioxide from being produced. Cutting the amount of carbon dioxide you produce will help to prevent global warming.

Your project

Y ou should now have enough information to carry out your own investigation into your local area. You will need to think carefully about the project that you want to do.

Students help to plant new trees as part of a coastal improvement project.

First of all, you need to choose your topic. You could look at how you can encourage **sustainable** development or stop climate change in your local area. For example, you could design a campaign to make your school or family more environmentally friendly. Help to set-up a **recycling** scheme or investigate how easy it would be to plan a safe cycle route to school. Remember, you should choose a topic that really interests you.

Sherlock Bones has built a compost heap in his garden. By collecting kitchen waste such as vegetable peelings and grass trimmings, then leaving them to rot in a box made from wooden slats, Sherlock Bones is able to not only reduce the amount of rubbish he creates, but now he has a handy supply of compost. Some local councils offer help with setting up your own compost heap – why not find out if they can help you?

Project presentation

- Design your own poster to publicize your project or campaign. Perhaps you could put it up at school.
- You could interview members of your school to find out their views on your campaign. You could record this on a video to make your own campaign documentary.
- Why not prepare a talk or assembly to present your ideas to the rest of your school?
- Keep a diary to record the problems or successes of your campaign. What could you do to overcome these problems?
- Involve your local council. You could invite a member of your local council to your presentation to make sure that they are aware of your views.
- How will your campaign carry on in the future when you have left your school? If you have a school council, you might want to discuss your plans with them. Alternatively, you could speak to your headteacher.

Children deposit glass for recycling in a bottle bank.

Members of Greenpeace (a well-known environmental campaign group) protest outside a site where rubbish is burnt. Smoke from the incinerator at the site could cause health problems for those living in the local area.

Glossary

Accessibility A measure of whether it is possible to reach, access, or move around a place or object.

Air mass A large body of air with a similar temperature and moisture content. It can extend for thousands of kilometres.

Carbon dioxide A colourless, odourless gas. It is formed when substances that contain carbon (like wood and coal) are burnt. It is also a greenhouse gas.

Cultural diversity The mix of people from different ethnic groups or cultures who live within a community or area.

Developed countries The wealthiest nations in the world, with a high standard of living. They include Western Europe, the United States, Canada, Japan, Australia, and New Zealand.

Developing countries The poor countries of the world that are currently trying to develop industry so that they can earn more money. They often have high levels of debt, which they owe to developed countries.

E-coli A type of bacteria found in the gut of birds and animals. It is needed to digest food properly, but if E-coli contaminates meat, it can cause severe illness.

Economic activity The work that people do to make money so that they can support themselves.

Enhanced greenhouse effect This effect is caused by greenhouse gases released by human activity (such as burning fossil fuels). It happens in addition to the natural greenhouse effect and leads to global warming and climate change.

Environmental (or ecological) footprint The mark that we leave on the planet and how our activities affect the environment. It is created by the way we live and includes things like the amount of water we use.

Fairtrade An agreement set up between farmers in developing countries and companies in developed countries. The agreement means that farmers get a fair price for their products. The money they earn is then used to invest in their local communities, to improve their quality of life.

Fertilizer A substance used to make plants grow better. Artificial fertilisers are manufactured from chemicals, and can cause pollution.

Food miles The distance that food travels before it reaches your plate.

Global positioning service (GPS) device A piece of equipment that communicates with satellites in space to tell you your exact location.

Global warming The trend towards the Earth gradually getting warmer. It is caused by the enhanced greenhouse effect. It is thought that global warming will cause freak weather patterns such as flooding and drought.

Greenhouse effect The heating that occurs when gases such as carbon dioxide trap heat escaping from the Earth and return it back to the surface. The gases act like the glass in a greenhouse, keeping the Earth warm.

Greenhouse gas A gas, such as carbon dioxide, that causes the greenhouse effect.

Ordnance Survey The organization set up by the government to produce accurate maps of the United Kingdom.

Population A group of people who live in an area.

Recycling Waste materials that are processed to turn them back into useful materials.

Rural An area in the countryside.

Salmonella A type of bacteria that causes food poisoning and is commonly found in meat and animal waste.

Settlement A place where people live.

Site The specific area where you choose to locate your settlement.

Sustainable The quality of the environment and how it can be maintained in the long term

Urban A built up area such as a town or city.

Weil's disease A disease spread by rat urine. It causes flu-like symptoms. It can be fatal if it is left untreated.

Answers

Page 4 Hotel 5331
Caravan site 5332
Information site 5132

Page 7 The world is shown as a flat circle, not a sphere. Jerusalem is shown to be at the centre of the world. The map contains strange descriptions of imaginary people who lived in unknown places.

Page 9 The castle was built in the eleventh century in the middle of a gap in a giant chalk ridge (hill) that stretches for many miles across southern England. It was an important place, because the people who controlled this location could control trade and the movement of people between the areas on either side of the ridge.

Page 15 You can feel these bumps when you walk over them. They warn people (especially those who have bad eye-sight) that there might be a road crossing ahead.

Page 19 They're all true!

Page 23 Foxes are a danger to pets (they have been known to kill cats and puppies). They overturn rubbish bins. They dig up garden lawns, foul school playgrounds and chew through cables.

Page 24 The congestion charge encourages people to use public transport (buses, trains, trams and the Underground). These forms of transport release less air pollution than if everyone travelled in their own car. This helps the UK to work towards meeting the targets set to reduce the amount of carbon dioxide we release into the air – carbon dioxide is one of the main gases that causes global warming.

Further information

Good detective work will help you to find out more about your local area. Your local library is a great source of information about local events, places and people. If you are trying to find out more about how your area or the people who live there have changed, you could try visiting your local church. They often have old records which could be excellent sources of information.

Books to Read

Exploring Seaside Towns by Katie Orchard (Wayland, 2005)

Exploring Villages by Katie Orchard (Wayland, 2004)

Sustainable World: Energy / Environment / Food and Farming / Transport / Urbanization / Waste by Rob Bowden (Wayland, 2003)

Index